Sassy Lassy

TRY NOT TO LAUGH CHALLENGE™

11 Year Old Edition

TM & Copyright© 2020 by Try Not To Laugh Challenge Group

ALL RIGHTS RESERVED.

Published in the United States. By purchase of this book, you have been licensed one copy for personal use only. No part of this work may be reproduced, redistributed, or used in any form or by any means without prior written permission of the publisher and copyright owner.

Try Not To Laugh Challenge
BONUS PLAY

Join our Joke Club and get the Bonus Play PDF!

Simply send us an email to:

➥ **TNTLPublishing@gmail.com** ➥

and you will get the following:

- 10 Hilarious BONUS Jokes
- An entry in our Monthly Giveaway of a $50 Amazon Gift card!

We draw a new winner each month and will contact you via email!

 Good luck!

Welcome to the
Try Not To Laugh Challenge
✨ Sassy Lassy Edition! ✨

RULES OF THE GAME:

★ Grab a friend or family member, a pen/pencil, and your comedic skills! Determine who will be "Lassy 1" and "Lassy 2".

★ Take turns reading the jokes aloud to each other, and check the box next to each joke you get a laugh from! Each laugh box is worth 1 point, and the pages are labeled to instruct and guide when it is each player's turn.

★ Once you have both completed telling jokes in the round, tally up your laugh points and mark it down on each score page! There is a total of 10 Rounds.

★ Play as many rounds as you like! Once you reach the last round, Round 10, tally up ALL points from the previous rounds to determine who is the CHAMPION LAUGH MASTER!

★ Round 11 - The Tie-Breaker Round.

In the event of a tie, proceed to Round 11. This round will be 'Winner Takes All!', so whoever scores more laugh points in this round alone, is crowned the CHAMPION LAUGH MASTER!

TIP: Use an expressive voice, facial expressions, and even silly body movement to really get the most out of each joke and keep the crowd laughing!

Now, it's time to play!

ROUND 1

Lassy 1

Why did the singer go to the doctor?
She needed an OPERA-tion!

LAUGH

What do you call it when an artist laughs?
Snicker-doodle.

LAUGH

How do pigs relax and unwind?
By taking a few swings in the HAM-mock.

LAUGH

What does a butterfly call its mom?
MOTH-er.

LAUGH

Lassy 1

Which weather condition is caused by multiple people thinking?
Brainstorm.

☐ LAUGH

What is a lawn mower's favorite song?
I'm sexy and I MOW it!

☐ LAUGH

Why did no one like black holes?
They are ABYSS-mal!

☐ LAUGH

What kind of club has no members?
A golf club.

☐ LAUGH

Pass the book to Lassy 2! →

Lassy 2

What is the flower's favorite singer?
BEE-yonce

How do you get more action and adventure while camping?
When it's in-tents!

What do mail and meat have in common?
SPAM.

What kind of car does a kitten drive?
A CAT-illac.

Lassy 2

Why was the soda so anxious?
He had so much bottled up!

◯ LAUGH

What do you call a unicorn with a bad attitude?
Uni-SCORN.

◯ LAUGH

Why did the flowerbed stay up all night?
It was GARDEN the house!

◯ LAUGH

How did the bicycle feel after reinflating her tires?
Pumped.

◯ LAUGH

Time to add up your points! →

SCORE BOARD

Add up each Lassy's laugh points for this round!

Lassy 1 — /8 Total

Lassy 2 — /8 Total

ROUND WINNER

ROUND 2

Lassy 1

What pasta is only worth one cent?
Penne.

 LAUGH

Why are mermaids considered to be vain?
They're always fishing for compliments!

 LAUGH

How does a mountain give a recap?
They SUMMIT all up!

 LAUGH

What camera equipment does an amateur photographer use?
TRY-pods.

LAUGH

Lassy 1

Why do bears hate elevators?
They get CLAWS-trophobic!

☐ LAUGH

Which fruit is thought to be the most caring?
PASSION-fruit.

☐ LAUGH

Why are painters never mad?
They just BRUSH it off.

☐ LAUGH

What do you call a big basketball player who got startled by a mouse?
Shaquille O'SQUEAL!

☐ LAUGH

Pass the book to Lassy 2! ➡

Lassy 2

Why was the root undefeated?
It simply couldn't be BEET!

☐ LAUGH

What do you call it when a computer has a large lunch?
A mega-BITE.

☐ LAUGH

Who is the pillow's favorite musician?
BED Sheeran.

☐ LAUGH

What did the minister say, when he watered his crop of greens?
"Lettuce spray!"

☐ LAUGH

Lassy 2

What's a snake's favorite musical?
MAMBA Mia. ☐ LAUGH

Why are frogs such good storytellers?
Their words are always so ribbeting! ☐ LAUGH

What is it called when a residence clutches something?
A house-hold! ☐ LAUGH

Why was the clarinet player kicked out of the library?
She was caught REED-ing. ☐ LAUGH

Time to add up your points! →

SCORE BOARD

Add up each Lassy's laugh points for this round!

Lassy 1   /8
              Total

Lassy 2   /8
              Total

ROUND WINNER

Lassy 1

What is icy yet still green?
Iceland.

☐ LAUGH

How does an eagle choose her manicurist?
She picks the most TALON-ted one!

☐ LAUGH

What's a gladiator's favorite meal?
CEASAR salad.

☐ LAUGH

Why did the girl take her binoculars to the supermarket?
She wanted to STALK the shelves!

☐ LAUGH

Lassy 1

What position do sea birds prefer to play in soccer?
Gullie!

LAUGH

Which phrase is good in basketball, but not in tennis?
"Nothing but net!"

LAUGH

What's the one requirement to get hired at a cannery?
A can-do attitude!

LAUGH

Did you hear about the man who lives with a pack of cheetahs?
SAFARI hasn't gotten eaten!

LAUGH

Pass the book to Lassy 2! →

Lassy 2

What did the geologist name his daughter?
Crystal. LAUGH

Why do athletes lie during warm-ups?
They like to stretch the truth! LAUGH

How did the girl explain meeting her boyfriend online?
"We just kind of CLICKED." LAUGH

What do you use to clean your trumpet?
A tuba cleaner! LAUGH

Lassy 2

Why are geese the worst drivers?
They're always honking!

LAUGH

Which Disney princess is the noisiest?
Belle.

LAUGH

How did the cell phone propose to his girlfriend?
He gave her a RING!

LAUGH

Why did the fruit fly travel to France?
He wanted to see PEAR-is.

LAUGH

Time to add up your points! →

SCORE BOARD

Add up each Lassy's laugh points for this round!

Lassy 1   /8
            Total

Lassy 2   /8
            Total

ROUND WINNER

ROUND 4

Lassy 1

What did the avocado say at the end of the play?
"BRAVO-cado!"

☐ LAUGH

How did the flower girl handle all her responsibilities for the wedding?
She really ROSE to the occasion!

☐ LAUGH

What do you call a musical about a baker?
The Greatest DOUGH-man.

☐ LAUGH

Why was the elevator the real MVP?
It worked hard on every level!

☐ LAUGH

Lassy 1

What did the table say to the legs?
"Without you, I'd be so BOARD." ☐ LAUGH

How do fairy musicians practice?
With a metro-GNOME! ☐ LAUGH

What's the best power tool to use at the beach?
The sander. ☐ LAUGH

How do you keep your prized pumpkin safe during the state fair?
You need to GOURD it carefully! ☐ LAUGH

Pass the book to Lassy 2! →

Lassy 2

Did you know that the other team lost the salad-making competition on purpose?
Apparently, they LETTUCE win!

☐ LAUGH

What do you call an alpaca's attorney?
LLAW-ma.

☐ LAUGH

Why is karaoke night down in the coal mines such a bummer?
Everyone is singing in MINER key.

☐ LAUGH

Which accessories are the loudest?
BANG-les.

☐ LAUGH

Lassy 2

What did the drama teacher say when none of her students had practiced their lines?

She told them to get their ACT together!

☐ LAUGH

Which pop artist loves to clean?

Taylor SWIFT-er.

☐ LAUGH

Which social media app do all clocks have?

Tiktok.

☐ LAUGH

Are you a pro with LEGO's?

Let's just say I've been around the BLOCK a few times!

☐ LAUGH

Time to add up your points! →

SCORE BOARD

Add up each Lassy's laugh points for this round!

Lassy 1   /8 Total

Lassy 2   /8 Total

ROUND WINNER

ROUND 5

Lassy 1

What kind of money do you use to buy coffee in space?
STAR-bucks.

Who is the most giving celebrity?
Ellen Da Generous.

What do you call a question mark with a bad attitude?
PUNK-tuation.

Why are yardsticks faster than humans?
Because they've got 3 feet!

Lassy 1

Which Disney movie do all carbs love?
PITA Pan.

LAUGH

What did the mama duck give her baby when he was sick?
Saltine QUACK-ers.

LAUGH

What is a hound dog's favorite midnight snack?
BEAGLE Bites.

LAUGH

What did the horse put on his spaghetti?
MARE-inara sauce.

LAUGH

Pass the book to Lassy 2! →

Lassy 2

What do you call candy that's naive?

Suckers.

Why do we never talk about old people's hair?

It's considered a gray area...

What kind of nut is the best at hiding things?

The pi-STASH-io.

Why do feet get so confused?

They can never shoes any options!

Lassy 2

What do flowers and dirt do on Valentine's Day?
Flirt.

☐ LAUGH

How did everyone know the two stitches were friends?
They were obviously close-knit!

☐ LAUGH

What did everyone in the pants family have in common?
Their JEANS!

☐ LAUGH

Why was the fisherman a good comedian?
He was always delivering one-liners!

☐ LAUGH

Time to add up your points! →

SCORE BOARD

Add up each Lassy's laugh points for this round!

Lassy 1 — /8 Total

Lassy 2 — /8 Total

ROUND WINNER

Lassy 1

Why did the boy have to join the school chorus?
It was a re-CHOIR-ment!

LAUGH

What do you feel when trees sneeze?
Woodwinds.

LAUGH

Can you make a wish on red fruit seeds?
Sure, your wish will be poma-GRANTED!

LAUGH

Why wouldn't the boat dock at the marina?
It harbored a grudge.

LAUGH

Lassy 1

Why did the phone go to the doctor?
It needed a screen-SHOT.

☐ LAUGH

How does the math tutor say goodbye?
"Calc-u-LATER!"

☐ LAUGH

What did the accountant do first when making his bed?
Spread-sheets.

☐ LAUGH

Why do carpenters get manicures?
To keep their nails in good condition!

☐ LAUGH

Pass the book to Lassy 2! →

Lassy 2

Why did the tree decide to get to know his neighbors?
He was finally ready to branch out! ☐ LAUGH

Which popstar likes to eat trees?
Justin Beaver. ☐ LAUGH

What do you call a rabbit-powered cooling system?
HARE conditioning. ☐ LAUGH

Why does no one understand what the shrub really wants?
Because he's always beating around the bush! ☐ LAUGH

Lassy 2

Why was the banana so upset?
He got bent out of shape!
☐ LAUGH

What set belongs to everybody and nobody at the same time?
The sunset.
☐ LAUGH

What did the green pepper say to the habanero?
"Wow, you look hot."
☐ LAUGH

How do cookies dance?
They do the Macaroon-a!
☐ LAUGH

Time to add up your points! →

SCORE BOARD

Add up each Lassy's laugh points for this round!

Lassy 1 — /8 Total

Lassy 2 — /8 Total

ROUND WINNER

ROUND 7

Lassy 1

What's a cat's favorite dessert?
Mice pudding.

☐ LAUGH

Why was the golfer always bankrupt?
It could never get out of the hole!

☐ LAUGH

What do you call a baby elephant?
Ele-INFANT.

☐ LAUGH

Why was the celery stick always sneaking around?
He liked to STALK.

☐ LAUGH

Lassy 1

What did the tulip ask the rose?
"Flower you today?"

◯ LAUGH

Which band gets nervous when driving through the city?
One Direction.

◯ LAUGH

Why does an astronaut like to have candles at the dinner table?
It really sets the atmosphere!

◯ LAUGH

What kind of tube offers hours of entertainment?
YouTube.

◯ LAUGH

Pass the book to Lassy 2! →

Lassy 2

Which dessert do all trees love?
The ROOT beer float.

☐ LAUGH

How did the cow react when she found out she was lactose intolerant?
She was in UDDER shock!

☐ LAUGH

What day of the week never loses?
WINS-day!

☐ LAUGH

Why did the bee stop getting invited to parties?
He was a real buzzkill.

☐ LAUGH

Lassy 2

What is Katniss' favorite food?
Peeta bread.

☐ LAUGH

Why did the teacher drink orange juice instead of apple juice?
It gave her more concentration!

☐ LAUGH

What did the tree say after the party?
"I'm gonna STICK around for a few more minutes!"

☐ LAUGH

Where did the turkey and ham first become friends?
At the MEAT-and-greet!

☐ LAUGH

Time to add up your points! →

SCORE BOARD

Add up each Lassy's laugh points for this round!

Lassy 1

/8
Total

Lassy 2

/8
Total

ROUND WINNER

ROUND 8

Lassy 2

What sport do evil stepmothers love the most?
BAD-minton.

☐ LAUGH

Why did the British people buy a house?
They wanted to own proper-TEA!

☐ LAUGH

What sport are people most suspicious about?
DODGE-ball.

☐ LAUGH

Why didn't the boy know how many pounds he was?
He didn't like giving anything a-WEIGH.

☐ LAUGH

Lassy 1

What do you call Selena Gomez covered in slime?
Selena GOO-mez.
☐ LAUGH

How do people know that you're an out-of-towner?
They see your tour-WRISTS!
☐ LAUGH

What do feet eat for breakfast?
TOE-st.
☐ LAUGH

What do you wear to a job interview to be an explorer?
A trail-BLAZER.
☐ LAUGH

Pass the book to Lassy 2! →

Lassy 1

What's the best way to get around a new town?
With a Jeep.P.S.

☐ LAUGH

Which bug likes to "swap" around letters?
Wasp.

☐ LAUGH

Did you hear about the failed time traveler with a big appetite?
She always went back four seconds!

☐ LAUGH

What do you call a naked fish?
BARE-acuda.

☐ LAUGH

Lassy 2

Which magical creature is the most selfish?
The Centaur of attention!

◯ LAUGH

How would you describe a charismatic BBQ?
CHAR-ming!

◯ LAUGH

What do you call a funny joke you heard on Disney channel?
A Dis-KNEE slapper!

◯ LAUGH

Which make-up product is guaranteed to help you study?
Highlighter!

◯ LAUGH

Time to add up your points! →

SCORE BOARD

Add up each Lassy's laugh points for this round!

Lassy 1   /8
                Total

Lassy 2   /8
                Total

ROUND WINNER

ROUND 9

Lassy 1

What did the ball say to the cat?
"Are you feline playful today?"

☐ LAUGH

Why couldn't the bears get along?
They were POLAR opposites!

☐ LAUGH

Which particle has the worst attitude?
Electrons, they're always negative!

☐ LAUGH

What did the blood-sucking bug say when he couldn't compete as a gladiator?
"I guess I'm just a hopeless roman-TICK."

☐ LAUGH

Lassy 1

What is a fairy's favorite drink?
Sprite.
☐ LAUGH

Why do knapsacks make for lousy friends?
They're always going behind your back!
☐ LAUGH

What's an artsy car's favorite thing on the highway?
The mile MARKERS.
☐ LAUGH

What kind of stash isn't hidden?
A mustache!
☐ LAUGH

Pass the book to Lassy 2! →

Lassy 2

Why isn't Antarctica considered to be smart?
It has 0 degrees.

LAUGH

I never trust the shadows. They always seemed a little shady...

LAUGH

What is the friendliest flower?
The HI-biscus!

LAUGH

Why did the cheese want to get a job?
He needed the extra cheddar.

LAUGH

Lassy 2

Which part of your body recovers fastest from injury?
Your HEEL. ☐ LAUGH

Why didn't the shark talk to the cute whale?
It was way out of his league! ☐ LAUGH

What do you call two small flowers that are always together in the garden?
Best Buds! ☐ LAUGH

Where do rodents live?
At their mouse pad. ☐ LAUGH

Time to add up your points! →

SCORE BOARD

Add up each Lassy's laugh points for this round!

Lassy 1 ___/8 Total

Lassy 2 ___/8 Total

ROUND WINNER

ROUND 10

Lassy 1

Why was the caterpillar a great attorney?
She really put in the legwork!

☐ LAUGH

Which car is known for having the best concentration?
Ford Focus.

☐ LAUGH

Why can't the shoes dance well?
They've got no SOLE!

☐ LAUGH

What advice should you give to a succulent?
"Cactus makes perfect!"

☐ LAUGH

Lassy 1

Why did the quarterback refuse help?
He usually made good PASSES!

◯ LAUGH

Why did the girl run her hairdryer in the freezer?
Her mom said she needed some dry ice!

◯ LAUGH

What is a soldier's least favorite month?
March.

◯ LAUGH

Why don't computers wear eyeglasses?
They already have contacts.

◯ LAUGH

Pass the book to Lassy 2! →

Lassy 2

What is an iPhone's favorite dance?
The MAC-arena!

 LAUGH

Did you see that one guy run through the library?
He was really booking it!

 LAUGH

What do you call pasta that always tells the truth?
FACT-eroni.

 LAUGH

Why do cups buy houses on the beach?
They always want to be by the coasters.

 LAUGH

Lassy 2

Which rock group do presidents love?
Mount Rushmore.

☐ LAUGH

Why was the guitar sad?
It was feeling over-worked and underplayed.

☐ LAUGH

What do you call an actor who cares?
A CARE-acter!

☐ LAUGH

What's a surgeon's favorite instrument?
The organ.

☐ LAUGH

Time to add up your points! →

SCORE BOARD

Add up each Lassy's laugh points for this round!

Lassy 1   /8
          ___
         Total

Lassy 2   /8
          ___
         Total

ROUND WINNER

Add up all your points from each round. The Lassie with the most points is crowned

The Laugh Master!

In the event of a tie, continue to Round 11 - The Tie-Breaker Round!

Lassy 1   _____ Grand Total

Lassy 2   _____ Grand Total

THE LAUGH MASTER

Lassy 1

What do sheep telemarketers say when you pick up the phone?
"Sorry to baaaaa-ther you, but..."

LAUGH

Why can't you trust a cosmetologist?
They make-up everything!

LAUGH

What's the smallest pole on earth?
The tadpole.

LAUGH

How did the boy know he was getting a cat as a present?
He had a good feline!

LAUGH

Lassy 1

Which kind of pool is not meant for swimming?
A pool table!

☐ LAUGH

Why are hockey players so shy?
They're always trying not to break the ice!

☐ LAUGH

What has a bridge but no water underneath?
A song.

☐ LAUGH

Who is the calmest celebrity in the world?
ZEN-daya.

☐ LAUGH

Pass the book to Lassy 2! →

Lassy 2

What do you call a brace made for an M&M?
An em-brace.
☐ LAUGH

How do you write a love poem for a baker?
You use lots of FLOUR-y language.
☐ LAUGH

Why did the stick man get in trouble?
He was DRAWN into it!
☐ LAUGH

What's always in the middle of lunch and dinner?
The letter N!
☐ LAUGH

Lassy 2

What do you call a sleeveless shirt that badly needs to be washed?
A stank top!

☐ LAUGH

How did they catch the ice cream shop bandit?
He CONE-fessed!

☐ LAUGH

What do you call a driving vacation in the fall?
Road TRIP.

☐ LAUGH

Which pop singer works in a salon?
Harry Style-ist.

☐ LAUGH

Time to add up your points! →

Add up all your points from the Tie-Breaker Round.
The Lassie with the most points is crowned
The Laugh Master!

Lassy 1 — /8 Total

Lassy 2 — /8 Total

THE LAUGH MASTER

Check out our

Visit our Amazon Store at:

other joke books!

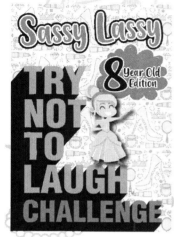
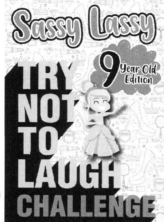
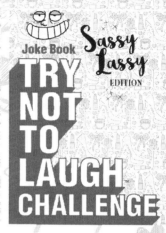
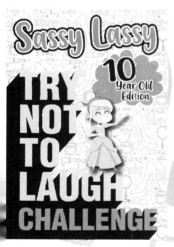

www.Amazon.com/author/CrazyCorey

Made in the USA
Monee, IL
25 March 2021